THE OFFICIAL
CELTIC
ANNUAL 2018

Written by Joe Sullivan
Designed by Chris Dalrymple

A Grange Publication

© 2017. Published by Grange Communications Ltd., Edinburgh, under licence from Celtic FC Limited. Printed in the EU.

Every effort has been made to ensure the accuracy of information within this publication but the publishers cannot be held responsible for any errors or omissions. Views expressed are those of the author and do not necessarily represent those of the publishers or the football club. All rights reserved.

Photographs by Alan Whyte and Ryan Whyte, Angus Johnston, Celtic Multi-Media, Shutterstock & Press Association.

Celtic logo is a registered trademark of The Celtic Football Club.

ISBN 978-1-911287-67-4

CONTENTS

CLUB HONOURS

Scottish League Winners [48 times]
1892/93, 1893/94, 1895/96, 1897/98,
1904/05, 1905/06, 1906/07, 1907/08,
1908/09, 1909/10, 1913/14, 1914/15,
1915/16, 1916/17, 1918/19, 1921/22,
1925/26, 1935/36, 1937/38, 1953/54,
1965/66, 1966/67, 1967/68, 1968/69,
1969/70, 1970/71, 1971/72, 1972/73,
1973/74, 1976/77, 1978/79, 1980/81,
1981/82, 1985/86, 1987/88, 1997/98,
2000/01, 2001/02, 2003/04, 2005/06,
2006/07, 2007/08, 2011/12, 2012/13,
2013/14, 2014/15, 2015/16, 2016/17

Scottish Cup Winners [37 times]
1892, 1899, 1900, 1904, 1907, 1908,
1911, 1912, 1914, 1923, 1925, 1927,
1931, 1933, 1937, 1951, 1954, 1965,
1967, 1969, 1971, 1972, 1974, 1975,
1977, 1980, 1985, 1988, 1989, 1995,
2001, 2004, 2005, 2007, 2011, 2012,
2017

League Cup Winners [16 times]
1956/57, 1957/58, 1965/66, 1966/67,
1967/68, 1968/69, 1969/70, 1974/75,
1982/83, 1997/98, 1999/00, 2000/01,
2005/06, 2008/09, 2014/15, 2016/17

European Cup Winners
1967

Coronation Cup Winners
1953

BRENDAN RODGERS

ON May 23, 2016, Brendan Rodgers stepped on to the hallowed turf of Paradise as Celtic manager for the first time as 13,000 Hoops fans proclaimed him almost as a homecoming son.

Just one year later, on May 27, 2017, the Irishman stood at the mouth of the same tunnel with the League Cup, the Premiership trophy and the Scottish Cup all wrapped up in green and white ribbons.

The manager had led his team to the treble, the first treble in 16 years and only the fourth in the club's history as he joined Jock Stein, twice a treble winner, and Martin O'Neill as the only managers to achieve this with Celtic.

Not only that, Brendan Rodgers led the Celts to all three trophies unbeaten as his Hoops finished the domestic season as 'The Invincibles', becoming the first team to achieve this feat.

The League Cup win, achieved with four straight wins, and Brendan Rodgers' first trophy win as a manager was also Celtic's 100th major trophy win.

The Premiership win was also Celtic's sixth in a row, the third time the club has achieved this and the unbeaten league win was only the second time the club had done this, the first being nearly 120 years previously when the champions of season 1897/98 won 15 and drew three of their 18 league games.

Brendan Rodgers' Hoops won an even bigger ratio of their games with 34 wins and four draws from the 38 league games and also created a new league record of 106 points and an SPFL record of 106 goals scored.

The Scottish Cup win came after five straight wins in which the Celts scored 17 goals for the loss of only two, St Mirren and Aberdeen being the only sides to score against the Hoops.

In the finals and semi-finals of both cup competitions the Celts beat both Aberdeen and Rangers, who were also their nearest challengers in the league, finishing second and third respectively, and the highlights of the league season for many would have been the 5-1 destructions masterminded by the Irishman both home and away over the Ibrox side.

He also led the Hoops to the group stages of the UEFA Champions League for the first time in three years amid a season of fantastic success.

On that first day at Celtic Park, he said: "I've been a Celtic supporter all my life and I'm very lucky now to have been given the opportunity to step out of the stands and on to the sideline and manage the team.

"So hopefully the supporters will understand that when you have that passion and emotion with the club, myself and the staff and the players will be doing absolutely everything we can to meet the challenges

that are set for us - that's to dominate here in Scotland and to qualify for the Champions League.

"For that we need them. This is an incredible football club, the support here is phenomenal and my idea is to get the stands filled again.

"In the last few years the top tier of the Lisbon Lions Stand has been closed or empty. It's my job to get over 60,000 people in here again and inspire the supporters to come back and watch a game of football that excites them and is about scoring goals and is about winning."

No one can say that Brendan Rodgers didn't deliver on his promises on all fronts.

MANAGER FACTFILE

D.O.B: 26/01/73
Born: Carnlough, Ireland
Playing career record:
Ballymena United (1987-90)
Reading (1990-93)
Newport (1993-94)
Witney Town (1994-95)
Newbury Town (1995-96)

As Manager:
Watford (2008-09)
Reading (2009)
Swansea City (2010-12)
Liverpool (2012-15)
Celtic (2016 to date)

Managerial honours:
League Champions (2016/17)
Scottish Cup Winners (2016/17)
League Cup Winners (2016/17)

SPOT THE DIFFERENCE

THERE are 10 differences in these pictures of Scott Sinclair in the thick of the Scottish Cup final action against Aberdeen. The first one has been circled, but can you spot the rest?

Answers on page 62.

THE CELTIC TROPHY MAZE

THE Scottish Cup has just been added to the League Cup and the SPFL Premiership to make the treble, but it has to make its way from Hampden Park to Celtic Park. Can you find the route to take the trophy to its home in Paradise?

START

FINISH

Find out how the Scottish Cup joined the other silverware in the Celtic trophy room on page 62.

JULY SEASON 2016/17

12	CL	0-1	v Lincoln Red Imps	
20	**CL**	**3-0**	**v Lincoln Red Imps**	**(Lustig, Griffiths, Roberts)**
27	CL	1-1	v Astana	(Griffiths)

(Home matches in bold)

THE arrival of Brendan Rodgers as manager delivered renewed hope of an exciting season in the drive for six-in-a-row and the arrival of Moussa Dembele and Kolo Toure added to the feel-good factor.

Even a surprise 1-0 defeat to Lincoln Red Imps in Gibraltar in the Champions League qualifiers on a synthetic surface barely averted the course and the following week on the lush green grass of Paradise, the Hoops eased to a 3-0 win and a 3-1 aggregate score over the European minnows.

Those games were played amid the traditional pre-season games, with the base camp this summer being in Slovenia and the first match was actually played in June – a 2-2 draw with NK Celje.

There were three other games before the Gibraltar trip, Sturm Graz (1-0), Olimpija Ljubljana (2-1) and Maribor (0-0), plus the Hoops also beat German side, VfL Wolfsburg 2-1 in a home friendly played between the two Red Imps matches.

The Hoops came out of the hat with Kazakhstan side, Astana in the next Champions League qualifier but the first leg fell between two other games as part of the pre-season build-up, though there was more of a competitive edge as the games were in the International Champions Cup.

In that tournament, English champions, Leicester City visited Celtic Park and the Hoops drew 1-1 with Claudio Ranieri's Foxes before travelling to Dublin to take on Barcelona, with the Catalan side winning 3-1 in the Irish capital.

In between those games, though, Celtic had made the nigh-on 6,000-mile round-trip to Astana where a Leigh Griffiths goal gave the Hoops a 1-1 draw.

AUGUST

SEASON 2016/17

3	CL	2-1	v Astana	(Griffiths, Dembele)
7	SPFL	2-1	v Hearts	(Forrest, Sinclair)
10	LC	5-0	v Motherwell	(Rogic 2, Dembele 2, Sinclair)
17	CL	5-2	v Hapoel Be'er Sheva	(Rogic, Griffiths 2, Dembele, Brown)
20	SPFL	4-2	v St Johnstone	(Griffiths, Forrest, Sinclair, Christie)
23	CL	0-2	v Hapoel Be'er Sheva	
27	SPFL	4-1	v Aberdeen	(Griffiths, Forrest, Sinclair, Rogic)

(Home matches in bold)

MORE new faces arrived during August with Scott Sinclair the first through the door followed by goalkeeper, Dorus de Vries and, right at the end of the month, Costa Rican defender Cristian Gamboa.

In the midst of seven competitive games in three different competitions, the Celts also played in their final game of the International Champions Cup when they lost 2-0 to Inter Milan in Dublin, but the month got off to an incredibly nail-biting start when a last-minute penalty from 20-year-old Moussa Dembele gave Celtic a 2-1 win over Astana for a tight 3-2 aggregate victory and progress to the play-off in the Champions League.

There was also drama in Celtic's opening league game against Hearts at Tynecastle when new Bhoy, Sinclair, made his debut from the bench and scored the winner in a 2-1 victory, and he was also among the scorers in midweek as the Hoops stylishly beat Motherwell 5-0 in the League Cup.

Celtic welcomed Israeli side Hapoel Be'er Sheva in the Champions League play-off and a 5-2 home victory looked comfortable enough until the second leg a week later when a 2-0 win for the home side made for a nervy 5-4 aggregate finish, but the Celts qualified for the cherished UEFA Champions League group stages.

The European progress was sandwiched by impressive 4-2 and 4-1 wins over St Johnstone and Aberdeen respectively as both James Forrest and Scott Sinclair kept up the happy knack of scoring in every league game so far.

SEPTEMBER
SEASON 2016/17

10	SPFL	5-1	v Rangers	(Dembele 3, Sinclair, Armstrong)
13	CL	0-7	v Barcelona	
18	SPFL	2-2	v Inverness CT	(Rogic, Sinclair)
21	LC	2-0	v Alloa Athletic	(Forrest, Dembele)
24	SPFL	6-1	v Kilmarnock	(Dembele 2, Forrest, Griffiths, Sinclair, Rogic)
28	CL	3-3	v Manchester City	(Dembele 2, Sterling og)

(Home matches in bold)

IN four home games in September, the high-flying Celts scored no fewer than 16 goals but, surprisingly, the fewest of that number were scored against Alloa Athletic in the League Cup with another clean sheet in a 2-0 win.

However, Rangers and Kilmarnock were put to the sword with 5-1 and 6-1 scorelines, with the first of those games setting down a marker for the rest of the season in Brendan Rodgers' first Glasgow derby as the Hoops tore Rangers apart. Moussa Dembele netted a perfect hat-trick and Scott Sinclair had now scored in the first four league games of the season, equalling the record of Stevie Chalmers that stood for 52 years.

14

THE TREBLE-WINNING INVINCIBLES

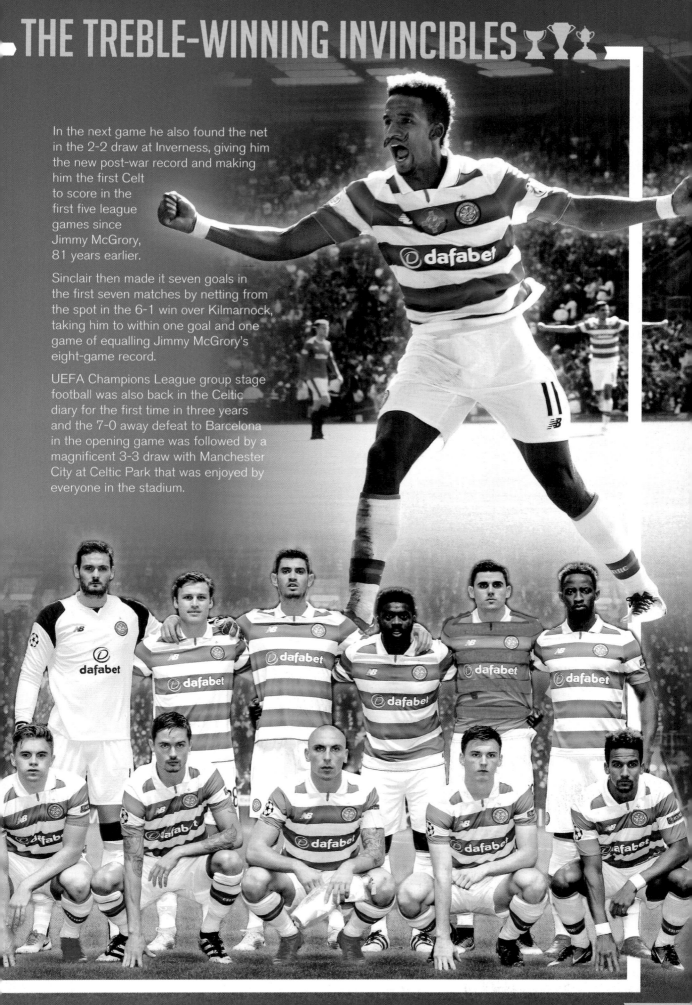

In the next game he also found the net in the 2-2 draw at Inverness, giving him the new post-war record and making him the first Celt to score in the first five league games since Jimmy McGrory, 81 years earlier.

Sinclair then made it seven goals in the first seven matches by netting from the spot in the 6-1 win over Kilmarnock, taking him to within one goal and one game of equalling Jimmy McGrory's eight-game record.

UEFA Champions League group stage football was also back in the Celtic diary for the first time in three years and the 7-0 away defeat to Barcelona in the opening game was followed by a magnificent 3-3 draw with Manchester City at Celtic Park that was enjoyed by everyone in the stadium.

OCTOBER

SEASON 2016/17

1	SPFL	1-0	v Dundee	(Brown)
15	**SPFL**	**2-0**	**v Motherwell**	**(Sinclair, Dembele)**
19	**CL**	**0-2**	**v Borussia Monchengladbach**	
23	LC	1-0	v Rangers	(Dembele)
26	SPFL	4-0	v Ross County	(Roberts, Armstrong, Sinclair, Dembele)
29	SPFL	1-0	v Aberdeen	(Rogic)

(Home matches in bold)

WHEN Scott Sinclair was replaced in the 84th minute by Stuart Armstrong, it was clear that he wasn't going to equal Jimmy McGrory's record of scoring in the first eight league games but a goal from Scott Brown at the start of the second half was all that was needed for another three points.

Sinclair did find the net in the following two league games, though, a 2-0 home win over Motherwell and a 4-0 win over Ross County in Dingwall. Those games sandwiched two matches in other competitions as the Hoops took on Borussia Monchengladbach in the Champions League and Rangers in the League Cup semi-final just days apart.

If the 2-0 losing scoreline to the German side wasn't a true reflection of how the game went thanks to Celtic's impressive display, the same could be said of the derby game as Moussa Dembele's goal was scant reward for Celtic's total dominance in a match which they mastered from start to finish.

The month ended with a potentially difficult trip to Pittodrie but a goal from Tom Rogic kept Celtic's unbeaten run on course and the Hoops finished October at the top of the league a full 11 points ahead of the pack.

NOVEMBER
SEASON 2016/17

1	CL	1-1	v Borussia Monchengladbach	(Dembele)
5	**SPFL**	**3-0**	**v Inverness CT**	**(Sinclair, Griffiths, Rogic)**
18	SPFL	1-0	v Kilmarnock	(Armstrong)
23	**CL**	**0-2**	**v Barcelona**	
27	LC	3-0	v Aberdeen	(Rogic, Forrest, Dembele)

(Home matches in bold)

ONCE more the month had games in three different competitions and after playing two games each in both the domestic and continental league formats, the Celts played their final League Cup game of the season and made it four wins out of four with no goals scored against them in the competition.

Aberdeen supplied the opposition, but, like in the semi-final against Rangers, they were swept aside by a rampant Celtic side as goals from Tom Rogic, James Forrest and Moussa Dembele ensured that not only had Brendan Rodgers won his first trophy as manager, but that the club had also lifted its 100th major trophy.

The win also maintained the Celts' unbeaten run domestically as the league games against both Inverness CT at home and Kilmarnock away on a Friday night were both won 3-0 and 1-0 respectively.

A fully-creditable 1-1 draw was earned in the away tie against Borussia Monchengladbach and even a 2-0 defeat to Barcelona couldn't halt the preparations for the League Cup final, and the month ended on that high with the first available silverware of the season.

DECEMBER SEASON 2016/17

3	SPFL	4-3	v Motherwell	(McGregor, Roberts, Armstrong, Rogic)
6	CL	1-1	v Manchester City	(Roberts)
9	SPFL	4-1	v Partick Thistle	(Armstrong 2, Griffiths, McGregor)
13	**SPFL**	**1-0**	**v Hamilton Accies**	**(Griffiths)**
17	**SPFL**	**2-1**	**v Dundee**	**(Griffiths, Bitton)**
20	**SPFL**	**1-0**	**v Partick Thistle**	**(Sinclair)**
24	SPFL	3-0	v Hamilton Accies	(Griffiths, Armstrong, Dembele)
28	**SPFL**	**2-0**	**v Ross County**	**(Sviatchenko, Armstrong)**
31	SPFL	2-1	v Rangers	(Dembele, Sinclair)

(Home matches in bold)

AS well as the final UEFA Champions League group stage fixture against Manchester City at The Etihad, Celtic could look forward to no fewer than eight SPFL games taking their tally to nine for the month of December.

The European tie came up second on the December schedule and once more Brendan Rodgers' Celts proved that this season's Champions League games had provided them with a valuable learning curve as they fashioned a 1-1 draw against the high-spending English side.

The month, however, got underway a few days earlier in an unforgettable game in which Motherwell were 2-0 and 3-2 ahead before the Hoops equalised to end a three-minute spell in which Celtic, then Motherwell, then Celtic again scored.

That was the 72nd minute and it stayed that way until the final minute when Tom Rogic did what Tom Rogic does best and fired in a last-gasp winner to make it 4-3 to the Hoops.

Another win quickly followed with a 4-1 victory over Partick Thistle on a Friday night at Firhill with two goals from Stuart Armstrong added to by Leigh Griffiths and Callum McGregor.

The first chance the club had to play at home since the League Cup final win, and the first domestic home game in five weeks, arrived with the first of three Celtic Park games in quick succession. They saw another three points with a 1-0 win over Hamilton Accies, thanks to a Griffiths goal, as the Celts continued unbeaten domestically despite losing both Kieran Tierney (Rangers, October 23) and Scott Sinclair (Barcelona, November 23), to game-consuming injuries.

The next game saw a 2-1 win over Dundee with Griffiths scoring in his third successive game but, a few days later against Partick Thistle at home, the winner in the 1-0 victory came from the returning Scott Sinclair in his first start after coming off the bench in the prior Dundee match.

JANUARY
SEASON 2016/17

22	SC	3-0	v Albion Rovers	(Sinclair, Dembele, Armstrong)
25	**SPFL**	**1-0**	**v St Johnstone**	**(Boyata)**
29	**SPFL**	**4-0**	**v Hearts**	**(McGregor, Sinclair 2, Roberts)**

(Home matches in bold)

CELTIC returned from their winter training camp in Dubai refreshed and ready for action. After seeing off Albion Rovers 3-0 in the Scottish Cup, the first league test of 2017 came against St Johnstone, and the Perth team were all that stood between the Hoops and equalling the Lisbon Lions' run of 26 domestic games unbeaten at the start of a season, which they'd set back in 1966/67.

It ultimately proved to be a tight game despite Celtic creating a number of chances, and it was a Dedryck Boyata header on 72 minutes which was enough to give Brendan Rodgers' side all three points, while the match was also significant in that it marked Scott Brown's 400th appearance for the Hoops.

Hearts were next up to try and stop Celtic from beating the club's 50-year-old unbeaten domestic record, but the Edinburgh club were swept aside at Paradise.

McGregor came into the starting line-up after Armstrong pulled up with an injury during the warm-up, and it was the midfielder who had the ball in the net first. Sinclair selflessly played McGregor through before he fired home with a clinical shot that went in off the post just before the half-hour mark.

Sinclair was next up, doubling Celtic's lead after he latched on to an inch-perfect ball from Kieran Tierney to put the Hoops 2-0 up midway through the second-half. Three minutes later, Tierney was the man with the creative magic again as he cut the ball back to Patrick Roberts who made it 3-0. Sinclair then stepped up to make it 4-0 with a cool penalty slotted home in injury-time.

FEBRUARY

01	**SPFL**	**1-0**	**v Aberdeen**	**(Boyata)**
05	SPFL	5-2	v St Johnstone	(Henderson, Dembele 3, Sinclair)
11	**SC**	**6-0**	**v Inverness CT**	**(Lustig, Dembele 3, Tierney, Brown)**
18	**SPFL**	**2-0**	**v Motherwell**	**(Dembele, Forrest)**
25	**SPFL**	**2-0**	**v Hamilton Accies**	**(Dembele 2)**

(Home matches in bold)

THE games were coming thick and fast in February, and Aberdeen were the first visitors to Celtic Park that month to face a Celtic side who lined up without Moussa Dembele, Stuart Armstrong and Leigh Griffiths.

And once again Dedryck Boyata was the match-winner as he headed home the only goal of the game from a Scott Sinclair free-kick just before the hour mark.

Four days later and Celtic were McDiarmid Park-bound to take on St Johnstone for the second time in two weeks. The Hoops took an early lead courtesy of Liam Henderson after six minutes, but that was cancelled out when Keith Watson equalised for the home-side. The Saints then went 2-1 up after David Wotherspoon's shot ricocheted off Boyata and into his own net.

Dembele entered the fray on 60 minutes, replacing Gary Mackay-Steven, and the Frenchman had an instant impact. A penalty was awarded in the 61st minute for handball against Watson, and Dembele stepped up to smash the ball high into the roof of the net to put the Celts back on level terms.

Fifteen minutes later Dembele was at it again with a low-drive from inside the box to put Celtic 3-2 up before Sinclair made it 4-2 inside the last 10 minutes.

The fifth goal was a sight to behold. Every Celtic player took a touch of the ball, as the play built up towards Mikael Lustig who pulled off a majestic rabona on the edge of the box, into the path of McGregor who flicked the ball in to Dembele to grab his hat-trick and 23rd goal of the season.

Not content with scoring a hat-trick against St Johnstone, Dembele repeated the feat the following weekend against Inverness Caley Thistle in the Scottish Cup as the Celts defeated their Highland opponents with room to spare as both full-backs, Lustig and Kieran Tierney, and skipper, Scott Brown, also got in on the scoring act.

And Dembele was on hand again to open the scoring against Motherwell in the next game, with Forrest scoring the second to restore the Hoops' 27-point lead at the top of the Premiership.

And Celtic's young French striker was the man with the goals again in the final game of the month, as he grabbed a brace against Hamilton in what was Celtic's 21st consecutive league victory.

MARCH

SEASON 2016/17

1	SPFL	4-0	v Inverness CT	(Sinclair, Dembele 2, Armstrong)
5	**SC**	**4-1**	**v St Mirren**	**(Lustig, Sinclair, Dembele, Griffiths)**
12	**SPFL**	**1-1**	**v Rangers**	**(Armstrong)**
19	SPFL	2-1	v Dundee	(Simunovic, Armstrong)

(Home matches in bold)

THE end was in sight as Celtic travelled to the Highlands to take on Inverness Caley, only seven points away from a sixth successive league title. However, there was no let-up from Brendan Rodgers' side or Moussa Dembele who bagged his second brace in as many games.

It was Scott Sinclair who was on the scoresheet first, though, with a magnificent goal just before half-time. Dembele doubled the Hoops' lead after a mistake from Caley keeper, Owain Fon Williams, which allowed the Frenchman to score just 12 seconds after the restart.

Armstrong whipped in a third before Dembele struck again in the 73rd minute to make it 4-0 with his 11th goal in five games.

Next up was more Scottish Cup action with St Mirren visiting for the quarter-final tie and the Paisley side took a shock lead in the 13th minute which they held up until just before the hour mark.

THE TREBLE-WINNING INVINCIBLES 🏆🏆🏆

It was then, however, that the Hoops struck twice in two minutes and then added another two for a 4-1 victory.

That was followed by a Glasgow derby which was dominated by Celtic. Armstrong gave the Hoops the lead in the first-half with his 11th goal of the season which was cancelled out three minutes from time by Clint Hill.

Griffiths was denied a stonewall penalty in stoppage time after he was brought down by Hill inside the box, while the Celtic striker also had a shot cleared off the line in the dying seconds of the game.

Nevertheless, the unbeaten run continued as the Hoops headed to Dundee looking for victory at Dens Park.

Jozo Simunovic fired Celtic ahead just before half-time and then Stuart Armstrong doubled the Hoops' lead early in the second half heading home a precise James Forrest cross, and it was a victory which put Celtic just one win away from being crowned champions of Scotland for the sixth consecutive season.

APRIL SEASON 2016/17

02	SPFL	5-0	v Hearts	(Sinclair 3, Armstrong, Roberts)
05	**SPFL**	**1-1**	**v Partick Thistle**	**(Sinclair)**
08	**SPFL**	**3-1**	**v Kilmarnock**	**(Armstrong, Sinclair, Forrest)**
16	SPFL	2-2	v Ross County	(Tierney, Roberts)
23	SC	2-0	v Rangers	(McGregor, Sinclair)
29	SPFL	5-1	v Rangers	(Sinclair, Griffiths, McGregor, Boyata, Lustig)

(Home matches in bold)

THERE were still eight games to spare in the league campaign when Brendan Rodgers' side clinched six-in-a-row in scintillating style away to Hearts at the start of April.

Scott Sinclair was again the scourge of the Tynecastle side, bagging a hat-trick for the Bhoys, with Stuart Armstrong and Patrick Roberts also finding the net in wonderful fashion. It was a fitting way for the Celts to cross the finishing line given their dominance of the league from day one and the sparkling football they had produced.

While the league crown had been secured, Celtic still had plenty to play for, most notably in the form of their unbeaten run which was extended to 40 games since the start of the season, as a 3-1 home success against Kilmarnock was bookended by draws against Partick Thistle and Ross County.

Celtic closed out the month with a Glasgow derby double header in which they ruthlessly stamped home their superiority over their city rivals. Goals in either half from Callum McGregor and Sinclair saw the Bhoys beat Pedro Caixinha's side 2-0 at Hampden in a completely one-sided Scottish Cup semi-final. Worse was to come for Rangers, however, the following week at Ibrox as the teams met in the league. This time the champions ran riot in a 5-1 trouncing, with Sinclair, Leigh Griffiths, McGregor, Dedryck Boyata and Mikael Lustig all on the scoresheet. It was a stunning showing from the Celts, and had they been more clinical, they could have dished out even greater punishment.

MAY SEASON 2016/17

06	**SPFL**	**4-1**	**v St Johnstone**	**(Roberts 2, Boyata, McGregor)**
12	SPFL	3-1	v Aberdeen	(Boyata, Armstrong, Griffiths)
18	SPFL	5-0	v Partick Thistle	(Griffiths, Rogic, Roberts 2, McGregor)
21	**SPFL**	**2-0**	**v Hearts**	**(Griffiths, Armstrong)**
27	SC	2-1	v Aberdeen	(Armstrong, Rogic)

(Home matches in bold)

EVEN without the suspended Scott Brown, who missed the first two matches of the month against St Johnstone and Aberdeen, Celtic maintained their irresistible form as a sensational season neared its climax.

A Patrick Roberts double helped sink the Saints 4-1 in Paradise on a memorable day for 18-year-olds Anthony Ralston and Mikey Johnston. Both players made their first competitive start for Brendan Rodgers' side against the Perth outfit, with Johnston making his Hoops bow, and their assured performances drew praise from the manager after the match.

After giving youth a chance at Celtic Park, the Irishman reverted to a more familiar-looking line-up away to league runners-up Aberdeen as the likes of Scott Sinclair and Mikael Lustig returned to the team.

It's always a tough test at Pittodrie but the Bhoys were quickly out of sight after a blistering start in which they scored three times in the opening 11 minutes. Dedryck Boyata made the breakthrough, while quick-fire goals from Stuart Armstrong and Leigh Griffiths left the hosts shell-shocked. To the Dons' credit, they did muster a response through an exquisite strike from Jonny Hayes but they couldn't breach a resilient Celtic rearguard again as the Hoops withstood an aerial bombardment to stretch their unbeaten run to a remarkable 44 games and reach the landmark of 100 points in the league.

Ladbrokes PREMIERSHIP

2016/17 CHAMPIONS

THE TREBLE-WINNING INVINCIBLES 🏆🏆🏆

With only two league games left to go to spoil Celtic's unbeaten run, the Hoops applied themselves resolutely in the final away game with a 5-0 win over Partick Thistle before bringing the curtain down on an amazing campaign with a 2-0 win over Hearts on Trophy Day in Paradise.

That left Aberdeen in the Scottish Cup final with Celtic aiming to further their Invincible tag by also going unbeaten in that tournament to deliver the club's fourth treble and the first in 16 years.

Jonny Hayes gave the Pittodrie side the lead after only nine minutes, but, just two minutes later with no Aberdeen player having touched the ball yet, Armstrong fired in from outside the area to equalise.

Celtic had the better of the game but it was still in stalemate until deep into time added on when Tom Rogic pounced with a last-gasp historic winner.

Celtic now truly were The Invincibles.

HOME TOWN BHOYS

MOST of you will know exactly where the Celtic stars hail from, but what do they think about where they were born? We find out here.

Moussa Dembele

I'm from Cergy-Pontoise, which is a small town outside Paris, around 20 minutes from the city centre. I go back home when there is an international break. When I'm not playing with the national team I have more time, but otherwise I go before I meet up with the squad.

Scott Brown

I'm from Hill of Beath in Fife but I don't get back that often. There's a grass park right across from my Mum's house, so we always played football on that. That's about it. That was what was in Hill of Beath at the time. I stay in Edinburgh now and the best thing about it is that it's quiet and not far from the beach.

Erik Sviatchenko

I'm from Viborg in Denmark. The city means a lot to me and it means more now than it did when I lived there and there are all the old memories when you go back. I moved away when I was 14 to FC Midtjylland and it still brings good memories back. It's a beautiful city with two big lakes in it so the nature there is lovely.

Stuart Armstrong

I was born in Inverness but schooled in Aberdeen so I would say I'm more Aberdeen than the Highlands. I don't get back as much as I would like. My family are away but my brother's still there, but I'm lucky if I'm up there twice a year.

Kieran Tierney

I was born on the Isle of Man but I only stayed there for about nine months. I then moved here but I try to go back as often as I can. Muirhouse is where I live and it's a place like no other. Everybody from there has been great with me.

Scott Sinclair

I'm from Bath and I try to get back as much as possible but it's hard because of all the games. It's historically significant because of the Roman Baths and it also has the Royal Crescent. It's not really an attraction or anything, it's just a place my friends and I used to go after school and hang out with each other.

Jozo Simunovic

My hometown is Zagreb. I have always lived there, and it's always nice to go back home. I go back at the end of the season, and if I don't get called up for the national team, I will go back for a couple of days. I like the city as it's very nice. I was born there and that city will always be in my heart. It's nice to come back as I grew up there. It feels familiar.

Craig Gordon

I was born in Edinburgh and I grew up in a village called Balerno. I went to school within a couple of miles of that but Edinburgh is my city and I still live within five miles of where I grew up. It's nice to be close to my family and that's one of the added benefits of playing up in Scotland with Celtic.

Cristian Gamboa

It's a small city in a province of Guanacaste called Liberia. I played football there when I was a kid in the lowest divisions and then in the first division. All of my family and all the people I know are from here. It's a really small place and it's close to the beach so it's in the middle of everything. It's a summer place where people go back home. It's really nice. Everything is there. Within 50 minutes you can go to the beach and in one hour you can go to the volcano where they get the spring water.

Nir Bitton

My hometown is Ashdod in Israel and I go back there every time I meet up with the national team, but I don't get to go there much on holiday. The best thing is that it's a beautiful city and has a beautiful beach. There are good people, good restaurants and it's a good life there.

PARADISE PROFILES

SCOTT BROWN

Position: Midfielder
Squad Number: 8
D.O.B: 25/06/85
Born: Hill of Beath, Scotland
Height: 5' 10"
Signed: 01/07/07
Debut: v Kilmarnock (h) 0-0 (SPL) 05/08/07
Previous Club: Hibernian

JAMES FORREST

Position: Winger
Squad: 49
D.O.B: 07/07/91
Born: Glasgow, Scotland
Height: 5' 9"
Signed: 01/07/09
Debut: v Motherwell (h) 4-0 (SPL) 01/05/10
Previous Club: Celtic Youth

CRAIG GORDON

Position: Goalkeeper
Squad Number: 1
D.O.B: 31/12/82
Born: Edinburgh, Scotland
Height: 6' 4"
Signed: 03/07/14
Debut: v St Johnstone. 3-0 (a) (SPFL) 13/08/14
Previous Clubs: Sunderland, Hearts, Cowdenbeath (loan)

MIKAEL LUSTIG

Position: Right-back
Squad Number: 23
D.O.B: 13/12/86
Born: Umea, Sweden
Height: 6' 2"
Signed: 01/01/12
Debut: v Aberdeen (a) 1-1, (SPL) 03/03/12
Previous Clubs: Rosenborg, GIF Sundsvall, Umea, Sandakerns SK

TOM ROGIC

Position: Midfielder
Squad Number: 18
D.O.B: 16/12/92
Born: Griffith, Australia
Height: 6' 2"
Signed: 09/01/13
Debut: v Inverness Caley Thistle (a) 3-1, (SPL) 09/02/13
Previous Clubs: Central Coast Mariners, Belconnen United, ANU FC

MOUSSA DEMBELE

Position: Striker
Squad Number: 10
D.O.B: 12/07/96
Born: Pointoise, France
Height: 6' 0"
Signed: 01/07/16
Debut: v Lincoln Red Imps (a) 0-1, (UCL) 12/07/16
Previous Clubs: Fulham, Paris Saint-Germain

SCOTT SINCLAIR

Position: Midfielder
Squad Number: 11
D.O.B: 25/03/89
Born: Bath, England
Height: 5' 10"
Signed: 07/08/16
Debut: v Hearts (a) 2-1, (SPFL) 07/08/16
Previous Clubs: Aston Villa, Aston Villa (loan), West Bromwich Albion (loan), Manchester City, Swansea City, Wigan Athletic (loan), Birmingham City (loan), Crystal Palace (loan), Charlton Athletic (loan), Queen's Park Rangers (loan), Plymouth Argyle (loan), Chelsea, Bristol Rovers

LEIGH GRIFFITHS

Position: Attacker
Squad Number: 9
D.O.B: 20/08/90
Born: Edinburgh, Scotland
Height: 5' 8"
Signed: 31/01/14
Debut: v Aberdeen (a), 1-2, (SPFL) 08/02/14
Previous Clubs: Wolverhampton Wanderers, Hibernian (loan), Dundee, Livingston

KIERAN TIERNEY

Position: Defender
Squad Number: 63
D.O.B: 05/06/97
Born: Douglas, Isle of Man
Height: 5' 10"
Debut: v Dundee (a) 2-1, (SPFL) 22/04/15
Previous Club: Celtic Youth

DEDRYCK BOYATA

Position: Defender
Squad Number: 20
D.O.B: 28/11/90
Born: Brussels, Belgium
Height: 6' 2"
Signed: 02/06/15
Debut: v FC Stjarnan (h) 2-0 (UCL) 15/07/15
Previous Clubs: Manchester City,
Bolton (loan), FC Twente (loan)

CALLUM McGREGOR

Position: Midfielder
Squad Number: 42
D.O.B: 14/06/93
Born: Glasgow, Scotland
Height: 5' 9"
Debut: v KR Reykjavik, 1-0 (a),
(UCL) 15/07/14
Previous Club: Celtic Youth

NIR BITTON

Position: Midfielder
Squad Number: 6
D.O.B: 30/10/91
Born: Ashdod, Israel
Height: 6' 5"
Signed: 30/08/13
Debut: v AC Milan (a) 0-2, (UCL) 18/09/13
Previous Club: FC Ashdod

PARADISE PROFILES

STUART ARMSTRONG

Position: Midfielder
Squad Number: 14
D.O.B: 30/03/92
Born: Inverness, Scotland
Height: 6' 0"
Signed: 02/02/15
Debut: v Partick Thistle (a) 3-0, (SPFL) 11/02/15
Previous Clubs: Inverness Caley Thistle,
Dundee United

JOZO SIMUNOVIC

Position: Defender
Squad Number: 5
D.O.B: 04/08/94
Born: Zagreb, Croatia
Height: 6' 3"
Signed: 01/09/15
Debut: v Ajax (a) 2-2 (UEL) 17/09/15
Previous Club: Dinamo Zagreb

ERIK SVIATCHENKO

Position: Defender
Squad Number: 28
D.O.B: 04/10/91
Born: Viborg, Denmark
Height: 6' 1"
Signed: 17/01/06
Debut: v Ross County (n) 1-3 (LC) 31/01/16
Previous Clubs: FC Midtjylland

EBOUE KOUASSI

Position: Midfielder
Squad Number: 88
D.O.B: 13/12/97
Born: Abidjan, Ivory Coast
Height: 6' 1"
Signed: 12/01/17
Debut: v St Mirren (h) 4-1, (SC) 05/03/17
Previous Clubs: Krasnodar, Shirak

JONNY HAYES

Position: Midfielder
Squad Number: 15
D.O.B: 09/07/87
Born: Dublin, Ireland
Height: 5' 6"
Signed: 19/07/17
Debut: v Linfield (a) 2-0, (UCL) 14/07/17
Previous Clubs: Aberdeen, Inverness Caley Thistle,
Cheltenham Town (loan), Northampton Town
(loan), Leicester City, Milton Keynes Dons (loan),
Forest Green Rovers (loan), Reading

DORUS DE VRIES

Position: Goalkeeper
Squad Number: 24
D.O.B: 29/12/80
Born: Beverwijk, Netherlands
Height: 6' 1"
Signed: 24/07/16
Debut: v Aberdeen (h) 4-1, (SPFL) 27/08/16
Previous Clubs: Nottingham Forest,
Wolverhampton Wanderers, Swansea City,
Dunfermline, ADO Den Haag, Telstar

PARADISE PROFILES

LIAM HENDERSON

Position: Midfielder
Squad Number: 53
D.O.B: 25/04/96
Born: Livingston, Scotland
Height: 6' 0"
Debut: v Motherwell, 5-0 (a) (SPFL) 06/12/13
Previous Club: Celtic Youth

PATRICK ROBERTS

Position: Midfielder
Squad Number: 7
D.O.B: 05/02/97
Born: Kingston upon Thames, England
Height: 5' 6"
Signed: 01/02/16
Debut: v Inverness Caley Thistle (h) 3-0 (SPFL)
20/02/16
Previous Clubs: Manchester City, Fulham

KRISTOFFER AJER

Position: Midfielder
Squad Number: 35
D.O.B: 17/04/98
Born: Raelingen, Norway
Height: 6' 5"
Signed: 01/06/16
Debut: v Lincoln Red Imps (h) 3-0 (UCL)
20/07/16
Previous Club: IK Start

JACK AITCHISON

Position: Striker
Squad Number: 76
D.O.B: 05/03/00
Born: Livingston, Scotland
Height: 5' 8"
Debut: v Motherwell (h) 7-0 (SPFL) 15/05/16
Previous Club: Celtic Youth

ODSONNE EDOUARD

Position: Striker
Squad Number: 22
D.O.B: 16/01/98
Born: Kourou, French Guiana
Height: 6' 1"
Signed: 31/08/17
Debut: N/A
Previous Clubs: Toulouse (loan), Paris Saint-Germain

ANTHONY RALSTON

Position: Defender
Squad Number: 51
D.O.B: 16/11/98
Born: Airdrie, Scotland
Height: 5' 11"
Debut: v St Johnstone (a) 1-2 (SPFL) 11/05/16
Previous Club: Celtic Youth

PARADISE PROFILES

CALVIN MILLER
Position: Striker
Squad Number: 59
D.O.B: 09/01/98
Born: Glasgow, Scotland
Height: 5' 11"
Debut: v Partick Thistle (h) 1-0, (SPFL) 20/12/16
Previous Club: Celtic Youth

MIKEY JOHNSTON
Position: Midfielder
Squad Number: 73
D.O.B: 19/04/99
Born: Glasgow, Scotland
Height: 5' 10"
Debut: v St Johnstone (h) 4-1, (SPFL) 06/05/17
Previous Club: Celtic Youth

JAMIE McCART
Position: Defender
Squad Number: 50
D.O.B: 20/06/97
Born: Law, Scotland
Height: 6' 2"
Debut: v Motherwell (h) 5-0, (LC) 10/08/16
Previous Club: Celtic Youth

CRISTIAN GAMBOA

Position: Right-back
Squad Number: 12
D.O.B: 24/10/89
Born: Liberia, Costa Rica
Height: 5' 8"
Signed: 30/08/16
Debut: v Barcelona (a) 0-7, (UCL) 13/09/16
Previous Clubs: West Bromwich Albion, Rosenborg, Copenhagen, Fredrikstad, Municipal Liberia

OLIVIER NTCHAM

Position: Midfielder
Squad Number: 21
D.O.B: 09/02/96
Born: Longjumeau, France
Height: 5' 11"
Signed: 12/07/17
Debut: v Linfield (h) 4-0, (UCL) 19/07/17
Previous Clubs: Genoa (loan), Manchester City, Le Havre

KUNDAI BENYU

Position: Midfielder
Squad Number: 26
D.O.B: 12/12/97
Born: London, England
Height: 5' 10"
Signed: 29/06 /17
Debut: v Linfield (h) 4-0, (UCL) 19/07/17
Previous Clubs: Aldershot Town (loan), Ipswich Town

FOOD FOR THOUGHT

EVER wondered what the Celtic players like to eat?
Well, we've asked for you and here are their answers.

Callum McGregor
Chicken Milanese - it is amazing. It's breaded chicken with pasta and a tomato sauce and I always get it from La Vita in Bishopbriggs. It's five minutes from my house and I'm there all the time.

Stuart Armstrong
I've been having home-made fried chicken recently so I'll go for that. It's nice and easy to make, just flour then put the batter on the chicken, nice and thin, it keeps it nice and crispy on the outside and moist in the middle. I've been trying to tell the boys about it but none of them are taking it on. I'm quite domesticated.

Kieran Tierney
Chicken curry, fried rice, salt and chilli chips, is my favourite. I don't get to have it often, though, maybe every week or two.

Jozo Simunovic

That's such a hard question because I love food! I mix it up all the time. The steak here in Scotland is brilliant, it's probably the best I've ever had.

Erik Sviatchenko

I don't really have a favourite meal, but my girlfriend and I use Gusto. I know Gary Mackay-Steven and Stuart Armstrong will laugh when they read this because I've been trying to get them on it. It's an online subscription to various meals — it's good quality and healthy too. I don't have a meal I'd choose every day, I like variation. I guess I like Tapas a lot, I like to share food.

Dedryck Boyata

I like pasta with pesto, pepper and chicken. I don't have any particular dishes I like. It's quite simple.

COLOURING-IN

HERE we have Scott Sinclair celebrating yet another Celtic goal. Use your crayons, ink markers or paints to bring Scott to full Celtic technicolour.

MIX-N-MATCH

See if you can match up the correct scores from last season to the correct team.

1. SPFL (H) 5-1

2. CL (H) 5-2

3. LC (H) 5-0

4. SC (H) 6-0

5. SPFL (A) 5-1

6. SPFL (H) 6-1

7. SPFL (A) 5-2

8. SC (H) 4-1

St Mirren

Rangers

Inverness CT

Rangers

Motherwell

Kilmarnock

St Johnstone

Hapoel Be'er Sheva

Answers on page 62.

THE INVINCIBLE LEAGUE CUP WINNERS

Brendan Rodgers delivers Celtic's 100th major trophy triumph

CELTIC went into the League Cup final having not lost a goal in the competition, and having played 15 domestic games without defeat – only a 2-2 SPFL draw at Inverness showing up on the debit side.

The club also went into the same game having won 99 trophies throughout its history and, with the 100th clearly in sight, Brendan Rodgers' first trophy as manager also made Celtic the Century Bhoys.

Along the way, Celtic had seen off Motherwell, Alloa Athletic and Rangers in the semi-final before beating Aberdeen 3-0 in the final.

It was an emotional Brendan Rodgers who addressed supporters outside Celtic Park following the success, which represented the first part of what would become a momentous domestic treble.

Later on, the manager said: "I was proud and happy that we'd gotten our hands on the trophy, but I was more pleased for the players, so that they could see that hard work pays off.

"The day itself was brilliant and I loved seeing the happiness all around. I was very proud to have delivered that trophy for Celtic and that's what I'm paid to do.

"The semi-final against Rangers was a stand-out game for me on the road to the final. Even though we dominated the game, it was 1-0, but we kept our composure and we kept playing.

"The players adapted to the adjustments that we had to make in the game, tactically, and eventually we ran out really strong winners.

"That was great. Then, of course, when we got to the final the plan was very simple – it was to go out on the pitch and arrive on that podium at the end with a good performance. Thankfully, we did that with a good performance and a 3-0 win."

THE INVINCIBLE PREMIERSHIP CHAMPIONS

Brendan Rodgers led his Celts to a historic title

WHAT more can be said about Celtic's six-in-a-row 2016/17 Premiership campaign? The facts speak for themselves. In Brendan Rodgers' first season in charge, quite apart from winning the League Cup, the Scottish Cup and making the group stages of the Champions League, the Hoops went through the campaign unbeaten, winning 34 of the 38 games played when even the four draws could easily be classed as unlucky not to win.

The unbeaten run hadn't been achieved by the club since the 1897/98 season when Willie Maley's side won the title without losing a single game in the 18-match campaign.

This, however, was more than twice as many games and, indeed, proved to be the club's most successful points ratio with the 93 per cent win beating the 90.4 per cent in Martin O'Neill's 2000/01 treble-winning campaign and, indeed, even the 91.7 per cent claimed by Willie Maley's Celts in 1897/98.

Brendan Rodgers' Invincibles also gained 106 points, beating the previous record of 103 that was set by Martin O'Neill's 2001/02 side, while they also netted an incredible new SPL/SPFL record of 106 goals – and they finished a full 30 points ahead of their nearest challengers.

It all started with a 2-1 win over Hearts at Tynecastle and it was at the exact same venue 29 games later that a 5-0 win clinched Celtic's sixth successive title.

And, just to add a certain sort of symmetry, the final game and Trophy Day was also against the Edinburgh side, this time in Paradise.

Brendan Rodgers said: "I think you only need to look at the fact that what we've done hasn't been achieved for more than one hundred years and that tells you how hard it is.

"It's a monumental achievement by the players, and there's a real dedication to excellence that's been shown since I came here.

"I arrived here on my first day – it was a lovely day – and having the supporters there was fantastic too. The trophy was there, but I hadn't won it. I had no involvement in it and what I wanted to do was go and win it, and until I did, I was never going to touch it. But, I can now and it's a great feeling."

	Team	P	W	D	L	F	A	GD	Pts
1	Celtic	38	34	4	0	106	25	+81	106
2	Aberdeen	38	24	4	10	74	35	+39	76
3	Rangers	38	19	10	9	56	44	+12	67
4	St Johnstone	38	17	7	14	50	46	+4	58
5	Hearts	38	12	10	16	55	52	+3	46
6	Partick Thistle	38	10	12	16	38	54	-16	42
7	Ross County	38	11	13	14	48	58	-10	46
8	Kilmarnock	38	9	14	15	36	56	-20	41
9	Motherwell	38	10	8	20	46	69	-23	38
10	Dundee	38	10	7	21	38	62	-24	37
11	Hamilton	38	7	14	17	37	56	-19	35
12	Inverness Ct	38	7	13	18	44	71	-27	34

THE INVINCIBLE SCOTTISH CUP WINNERS

THE oldest trophy in world football was all that was needed to complete Celtic's domestic treble, as well as truly making Brendan Rodgers' 2016/17 Hoops the Invincibles.

Once more, as they had done in the League Cup final as well as finishing behind Celtic in the SPFL campaign, Aberdeen were the challengers and yet again it was the Hoops who came out on top.

The side from the Granite City took the lead in the ninth minute but, within two minutes, and without any opposition player touching the ball, Celtic equalised through Stuart Armstrong.

Celtic were the dominant outfit but it wasn't until time added on that, as a fork of lightning flashed across a dull Glasgow sky, Tom Rogic surged into the box from the right and intricately sealed the 2-1 win.

Celtic had gone through the entire domestic season unbeaten and lifted the League Cup, the Premiership trophy and now the Scottish Cup – the club's fourth treble and the first for 16 years.

Brendan Rodgers had joined Jock Stein, who achieved the feat twice, and Martin O'Neill in the Celtic treble-winning managers' club.

Celtic had defeated Albion Rovers, Inverness CT, St Mirren and Rangers on the way to the final with only the Paisley side scoring against them on the way.

Brendan Rodgers said: "We're elated. It was a very tough game and, obviously, to win it the way that we did was special.

"It's an incredible feeling and full congratulations to the players. I'm just glad the lightning didn't strike Tom before he had his shot! Maybe the stars aligned for us this year but there's just been a feeling about this season. Don't get me wrong, we've had to earn it and we've had to work hard.

"We went into a big week when we played Rangers in the semi-final and we were exceptional. Our control and possession was really first-class and we deserved to get to the final.

"It was an incredible week for the Celtic supporters, as well as for the players and manager. To beat your biggest rival at Hampden so convincingly was really pleasing, and I think it set a tone for the week leading up to the league game.

"People might have expected Rangers to be angry from losing out in the Scottish Cup and to want to put that right at home, but for us to go there and bring an even better performance, and to create history on the day by being the first Celtic team to score five goals at Ibrox, really showed the level that the players produced that week."

DOT-TO-DOT

JOIN up all of the dots and see if you can identify what the Celtic image is.

Solution on page 63.

2016/17 TREBLE-WINNING QUIZ

1. WHO WERE THE ONLY TWO CELTS TO SCORE IN ALL THREE DOMESTIC COMPETITIONS – AND EUROPE?

2. WHICH PLAYER SCORED CELTIC'S FIRST GOAL IN THE LEAGUE CAMPAIGN?

3. WHO WAS CELTIC'S TOP LEAGUE CUP SCORER?

4. WHAT WAS SPECIAL ABOUT THE LEAGUE CUP WIN?

5. WHICH PLAYER SCORED CELTIC'S FIRST GOAL IN THE LEAGUE CUP CAMPAIGN?

6. HOW MANY GOALS DID CELTIC SCORE IN ALL THREE COMPETITIONS?

7. WHO WAS CELTIC'S TOP LEAGUE SCORER?

8. WHICH SIDE DID CELTIC SCORE MOST GOALS AGAINST IN THE DOMESTIC COMPETITIONS?

9. WHO WAS CELTIC'S TOP SCOTTISH CUP SCORER?

10. WHICH PLAYER SCORED CELTIC'S FIRST GOAL IN THE SCOTTISH CUP CAMPAIGN?

Answers on page 63.

HEROES' HEROES

Loads of youngsters look up to the Celtic players, but who are the role models for the Bhoys? Here are some of their answers.

Stuart Armstrong

I'm a big admirer of Muhammad Ali. I just like his story and his approach to fights in the way he built himself up and then produced the wins at the back of it. It's not dissimilar to what Conor McGregor is doing, but Ali was the first to do it and he won his fights with such style.

Kieran Tierney

Conor McGregor. I admire his mindset and everybody knows what he's about. His positivity as well, and it's really great for athletes to look up to. I met him last year and spoke to him for 10 minutes. Even that was inspirational for me. I was star-struck, that's the only person I could say I was properly star-struck with. I didn't even really know what to say to him.

Erik Sviatchenko

My Father, Sergei Sviatchenko. He's done so much for his family, especially when he moved to Denmark with just one suitcase following the collapse of the Soviet Union in 1990. He was educated as an architect but really wanted to make his living as an artist and he did. He's been accepted all around the world. He's been so successful and still is. He's given us a life that we could only dream of. I admire him, both my parents actually, for their persistence in giving us the life we have now.

Jozo Simunovic

I don't really have an idol or someone I look up to. For me, the most important thing in life is fate and God. It gives me peace and makes me stronger.

Dedryck Boyata

There's no-one in particular that I can think of. In terms of sportsmen, I like the boxer, Floyd Mayweather. He's a very confident person. I don't know if I'd like to be like him but I do admire him.

DEFINE INSPIRATION

THE Celts certainly have plenty of driving force on the pitch but we asked what really motivates them in their everyday lives.

Kieran Tierney

My family. I just like to give back to them what they've always given me - giving me lifts everywhere, taking me up and down to training. My big sister as well. She's four years older than me, but the older I get, the closer I get to her. Most things I do are for my family.

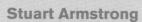

Jozo Simunovic

I would say it's the fact that I'm hungry to be better every day. That pushes me on, even when I'm so tired, I just try to get through that and be better. That's what inspires me, just to keep getting better and be as good as I can possibly be every single day.

Stuart Armstrong

Perspective. I think sometimes the football world can get a bit much when it's not going as you'd like it to with the pressure and the things that come with it, so it's important to remember other things that other people are doing and where you are and the benefits that come from football.

Callum McGregor

It's easy to say football but it's always been the biggest part of my life. I have met so many really good people in football and learned from them. Mark Fotheringham was a big influence on me at Notts County, taking me under his wing, and I would have to say my Mum and Dad as well as they have always looked after me and been a big influence on me. I also admire people that can speak different languages and it inspires me to push myself to try and do it.

HOOPS ON HOLIDAY

WHEN the players get a break, they all have their favourite vacation destinations and we asked them for their favourites.

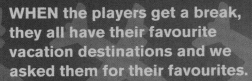

THE MALDIVES

FLAMINGO

Nir Bitton

The Maldives. The people there are very nice, it's very chilled. You don't have malls to go to or shops, you just chill in your room or at the pool. It's very nice.

Cristian Gamboa

It would be back home and going to Flamingo or Tamarindo beaches which are around 45 minutes away. I have a cousin who lives there and it's really nice to go there and chill with him on the beach, relax and enjoy the sun. They are very natural beaches. A lot of people go to Tamarindo and it can get really busy but Flamingo is quieter.

Stuart Armstrong

It's a fine line between New York and the south of France. Anything you could ever imagine is in New York and it's just a spectacular place. You could never be bored there. In the south of France the weather's just right. It's not too hot, not too cold, it's green and it has nice beaches. It's nice and calm.

Scott Brown

Dubai. It's absolutely roasting and they do everything. Whatever you want they're willing to get for you or they already have it. I've been a few times now.

Craig Gordon

Dubai, it's nice and warm and it's got everything you want to relax on holiday. It's a great family destination. You can go there and enjoy yourself as there are water parks, there is the beach and the sea has a warm temperature. It's easy to go there, relax and have a good time.

NEW YORK

DUBAI

Erik Sviatchenko

Either Paris or London, because Anne and I like the feeling of seeing different things, going to see cultural things and do a bit of shopping. We were in Barcelona where you can combine both things as Barcelona has the beach and the weather as well. So while I would say cities, at some point we have talked about going to the Maldives and doing nothing but relaxing, though I think we would get bored at some point so that's why we always go for a city.

Kieran Tierney

I went to Tenerife with my pal Jamie for 10 days and it was a great holiday. We were devastated about going home. Normally after 10 days you maybe want to go home but we had no sign of that. We loved it. We sat at the pool most days and at night we didn't go to any clubs or that because we don't drink so we just went to an Irish bar that had live music and karaoke.

Jozo Simunovic

I didn't travel a lot when I lived in Croatia because there we had everything. You have winter and summer tourism. From Zagreb, it's only an hour-and-a-half drive and you are at the sea along a big coastline. I didn't travel a lot outside the country apart from visiting my Grandparents in Bosnia, but usually I was in Croatia for summer or winter. I would never go to the same place in Croatia two years in a row but my favourite island is Mali Losinj.

Scott Sinclair

It'd have to be the Maldives. I've only been there once but it's just a place you can chill and with us having a little one now I don't think I'll be able to do that much. Me and Helen went there a few years back so I'd probably go back. It's pure relaxation, it was unbelievable. It's perfect if you've got a hectic lifestyle.

Moussa Dembele

My favourite holiday destination is going back to Mali to see my family. My Dad's family are from a small village called Kobiry. It's about four hours from the capital. I haven't been there for a long time but I'm planning to go there very soon. Apart from that, it would just be going back home to Cergy.

SIX-IN-A-ROW

BRENDAN Rodgers led the Hoops to their sixth successive championship last season in the most convincing success of all 48 of Celtic's titles.

Here we take a look back at all six consecutive trophy days and the facts and figures from the top of the tables.

ONE - 2011/12

		P	W	D	L	F	A	GD	Pts
1	Celtic	38	30	3	5	84	21	+63	93
2	Rangers	38	26	5	7	77	28	+49	73
3	Motherwell	38	18	8	12	49	44	+5	62

TWO - 2012/13

		P	W	D	L	F	A	GD	Pts
1	Celtic	38	24	7	7	92	35	+57	79
2	Motherwell	38	18	9	11	67	51	+16	63
3	St Johnstone	38	14	14	10	45	44	+1	56

THREE - 2013/14

		P	W	D	L	F	A	GD	Pts
1	Celtic	38	31	6	1	102	25	+77	99
2	Motherwell	38	22	4	12	64	60	+4	70
3	Aberdeen	38	20	8	10	53	38	+15	68

FOUR - 2014/15

		P	W	D	L	F	A	GD	Pts
1	Celtic	38	29	5	4	84	17	+67	92
2	Aberdeen	38	23	6	9	57	33	+24	75
3	Inverness CT	38	19	8	11	52	42	+10	65

FIVE - 2015/16

		P	W	D	L	F	A	GD	Pts
1	Celtic	38	26	8	4	93	31	+62	86
2	Aberdeen	38	22	5	11	62	48	+14	71
3	Hearts	38	18	11	9	59	40	+19	65

SIX - 2016/17

		P	W	D	L	F	A	GD	Pts
1	Celtic	38	34	4	0	106	25	+81	106
2	Aberdeen	38	24	4	10	74	35	+39	76
3	Rangers	38	19	10	9	56	44	+12	67

PUZZLE ANSWERS

PAGE 8 – SPOT THE DIFFERENCE

PAGE 9 – MAZE

PAGE 47 – MIX 'N' MATCH

1. SPFL (H) 5-1   Rangers
2. CL (H) 5-2   Hapoel Be'er Sheva
3. LC (H) 5-0   Motherwell
4. SC (H) 6-0   Inverness CT
5. SPFL (A) 5-1   Rangers
6. SPFL (H) 6-1   Kilmarnock
7. SPFL (A) 5-2   St Johnstone
8. SC (H) 4-1   St Mirren